copy/body

maryan nagy captan

EMPTY{ }SET
PRESS

2017

Edited by Angelo Colavita
Cover art by William Lukas

1

he orders you to drop the sewing pins
their tips metallic and candy-like
from the fourth floor window
while your family celebrates below.

she turned one today
the yard is littered with pink.

your relatives
a familiar shade of lobster
prattle on in pairs.

this party is hers
this adoration is hers
the cake with her name on it.

he has stolen the pins from
your grandmother's kit:
a tannish woven basket
frayed with a broken latch.

you drop the pins into the crowd
like kamikaze pilots,
trusting gravity's intentions
and aiming at no one in particular.

2

when he was born
your mama poured
every ounce of
pluck
into raising him
up right.

an unshakable ray
aimed at his chest,
scanning each hiccup
and turtle-lipped yawn.

3

to pacify the sting,
you push the blood
between your teeth,
a smear of pink, faint
on your lower lip.
he pulls back his hand,
the flow now ferocious,
his blood drizzling into
the grass beneath you.

he has taught you the act of vanishing,
the art of mischief,
has secured your place
in family history as co-conspirator,
as Troubled Shadow.

4

in a game of tag,
you are always *it*.
you must get rid of whatever it is,
but *it* is you.

5

dressed in summer sweat and finally at the lake, he presents
the object. on the way to the lake, the object remains
hidden. you wonder if it's the toaster, you wonder if it's the
telephone, you wonder if it's a pack of gum or your father's
gun or the screws from your rocking chair that he'll throw
into the lake and now the joke's on you.

her doll is not new but a hand-me-down. it is wearing lace, a white christening gown speckled with mud. its shape leaves an imprint, wet on his back.

"You should cut the hair off," he grins, holding out the pair of shears from the shed.

you reach for the doll, squeeze the middle hard to make certain he can't yank it back. he can tell you're not convinced, your brows cartoonishly knit. he knows you; he knows how you buckle, what triggers the tears.

the grass by the lake is long, it scratches and houses bloodthirsty demons. you slap your shin, you slap your collarbone, you slap your chest, it echoes, you slap your temple, twice. this wilderness is feral. you swear the scissors nearly catch fire in the sunlight. the lake water must be boiling, its fish now ghosts.

6
when you were born,
her love like cell division
split and split again
as he looked on.

7
you are drawn to the tone of his laughter
you wince and rue and crave
a sardonic approval.

he tells you his mattress is stuffed
with hundreds,
a million sacks of coins.

your grandmother fears he'll split concrete
with his stomp,
begs her god for mercy.

where did he *learn* this?

you are too young to ask better questions,
to think past your father.
perhaps the answer *is* your father.

he carries on.

8

you imagine you are running away from home, that the
house itself is *it*. you pretend that he has taken the lead to
guide the two of you to freedom, the home away from
home. the smell of bacon encircles the yard. the lawn is
newly mowed with bits of grass collecting on your sneakers.
your sister watches from a distance with legs so small she
couldn't keep up if you ran on your knees. it is nearly lunch
time.

he runs you around for such a long while,
your breathing labored and polluting your play.
when you tag his dampened back,
you are breathless.

but in the curl of his lip, he is ready to retaliate.
it is always a game of retaliation.

he does you the favor of a ten second head start.
you are breathless.
he shoves you to the ground,
a hard deliberate tag that tangles your braids.

you are distraught,
the bacon is burning,
you can smell that it has charred,
the air now soiled.

you are overwhelmed by his limbs,
the grass clippings in your hair and mouth.

your sister takes note of the scuffle
as the sweat drips off of his nose and onto yours.

9

he dares	you to eat the play doh, to try it
he dares	you to place one of the legs
	onto your tongue
	the harvestman limping in the dirt
he dares	you to pluck
	the blinking light off
	the firefly
	place it onto your tooth
	and you do it and then do it again
	the next day to make your cousin laugh
he dares	you to stick the sewing pin through
	the tough skin of your finger
	now do it 9 more times
he dares	you to
he dares	you to
he dares	you to but
he dared	you to

10

you learn that human beings need oxygen to survive and entertain the idea of shutting off the air in your bedroom, locking the door and sealing the three of you inside. you and your sister will breathe fine, you've found a way to extract the oxygen that brothers need from your own. first, he will wake up coughing then he will turn blue and then he will vanish into thin air.

re
lease
the
  hold
to
catch
the
ex   tended
      hand

carefully
the tender
begins
    to pull.

it is impossible to discuss the question of
how thin the air should be in order to talk
calmly.

I do not think
about what home is,
self-possession or cold courage.
I do not have kids or husbands.
"it's just me," I say,
we round a bend.

the squirrels creak a rhythm
for the forest.
first a sandpiper,
then a loon.
Kyle tells me
the trees rub in commotion,
Joey mans the stern.

it has been stated too loosely
that a person should wait to digest the cedar
before going into water.

but the nerves remain capsized
in the bog,
the lens cap
sinks
to the bottom;
the fly now a part
of him.

phantom canoes,
they recede into the brush. I rinse
my fingers of the city
and adopt:
a rock for a pillow
roots for a bed,
but I do not rest there.

I do not bait the hand that feeds me,
it is shaped like my mother's
and armed with her rings.

I left the window open,
I left the stove on,
I left the fumes for you,
to breathe in,
to remember
to take care of the things
I neglect.

you will know me
better
than every neighbor
I've ever had.

you will know my
freckle count,
the burning in my skin,
keep tabs
on the strands
that clog the sink
and sink
your prints
into my limbs.

I stopped once
to catch my breath
the blue hornet nest
arrhythmic in my chest.

you stopped twice
to secure my certainty,
guided my shoulders
and gave way
to a mild confusion:
a favor.

hand
over hand
over hand
over hand
we ward off lung loss.

we chase demons the shade of ivy
then sit-fidget in your broke down car:
an inevitability
with the worst timing.

Inevitability
has the worst timing.

I left the water dripping,
I left my shoes in the sink,
I left the lilt of my voice
outside
in the leaves.

oh, my beloved,
my earworm,
my magic spark,
for as handsome as you are
and as sweet as this song,
I can swim circles around the score,
tread water with lead feet.

you murmur words
off book,
trace highways
to connect
my tummy
to my back.

I left the garden untended:
the weeds grew
over
and over
and over
and over
staining green with yellow,
undone and wild.

I left the grey in my hair
I left my scarf
in an airport
we will never go again

but this haircut,
it sticks to my cheeks.

I lie about the stove
I lie about my voice
I lie about sitting outside
I let you believe that
I am not wearing make up
that these circles are not
a mishmash
of too many nightmares,
of anxiety over doing the wrong thing.

I lie about my shoes
I lie about my posture
I lie about cleaning my room

but this relationship,
it puddles
into dialogue.

we riff on astronomy,
and you mock my showmanship.
I swear by your stories,
and you grasp at the passenger's seat.

a wrinkle
a time in space
i trace sharpie
across the lines of your face.

we age this way,
knob-knuckled,
our big toes
pointing further from north.

you wonder
about the men you've slept with
about women who call lovers *lovers*
and think,
is one more too many?

Expect nothing and you will never feel again.

you are worth more than
a pint for a thank you,
your gendered cursive
bending inexplicable.

Fear nothing and you will never sleep again.

but this voice
it will not carry
so you must teach the cat to speak in tongues.

pennies as worthwhile as bottle caps
speckle the jar of your body.

i trace sharpie
across the lines
of your chest,
sternum
sturdy
sunspots—
my speckled egg.

we build a home in a bottle
vibrate our distant futures
unhinge doors with bare paws
lock jaws and sing elvis
smoke weed and sing elvis
the floorboards doubled over and moaning—
this house is a haunt
black cat & broom
fog rising through the dust,
the doorknob waits.

there are characters in fiction
that have not died
they do not get sung the happy birthday song
but you wonder
if they imagine
their death:
Morticia Addams,
Scout,
and think,
will this be the bed i die in?

white knuckled beneath the sheets,
a means to reach
a burgeoning salvation

you explain it
as this:

a consciousness
for otherness

for other things
inexperienced

a mid-day
fever dream
spent

tossing diamonds around your tongue.

you a girl
you a woman
you a lady
tailored to me
slit from the same cloth
sore in all the right places

you a girl
you a woman
you a lady
fold intwo
tilting above

keel at the sense of
sharp hip burn
hum synonymical
weighty in purse
and pocket

you a girl
you a woman
you a lady
hold my hand
cupped
not laced
i will lead
i have verbed
hush strait throat
lips limelit

attention
to pay,

mind
to pay,

you a girl
you a woman
i will run
tip along slit
tailored to me
torn lace cupped
tilt hip up
i will right
you
in all
the sore places.

you a murmur
a capsize come
a thin wrist coo

an unkempt coop,
housing soft
egg-laying feathers.

seamless,
in filth,
we run the right gamut.

four bullet-sized pins
a whole split in two
a scar
 a scar
a scar
 a scar
raised and yellow
scabbed over awkward
a skin-stained aftermark

yanked thread caught on
caddy-corners from ten inch pins sown in and
surgically inserted to hold the bones in place.
loose thread yanked
a scar's new scar
cross-legged sitting
creates a deepened dip
in the first
creates a crease
in the second
creates a wrinkle
in the third
creates a cellulite wave
in the fourth.

a clatter of limbs
the pop of readjusted bones
and the high of the reconnect

a clutter of ribs
organs pushed to corners

all of it is shifting
is sloughing off
my body is younger
it feels muddier
and at the hands of a chiropractor
it bunches and rolls.

I feel touched by the shape of things
the curve of a hip
the arc of chapped, wetted lips
eyelash crescents stuck to flushed, freckle-pocked cheeks.

and the way a belly puffs out,
dimpled and covered with hair,
rock solid up top
and soft and squished at the waist of my pants.

copy/body

maryan nagy captan

EMPTY{ }SET
PRESS

2017

I
the body
the bodies
they jam to a collective sway
each its own
yet never an individual

II
the body
a language scarred
stuttered and shaped by cotton
it wraps around the bar,
a phallacy,
oiled by disparate hands.

III
a fist full of pennies
crammed in a tin.

IV
if you stick your finger in your mouth
you can swipe the lipstick clean.

V
the nerve of her mother
(a dire in straits)

VI
the body
it stands alone
bathed in the brevity of a windowed glint:
a lilac sans sunlight.

VII
money ready hellos
breath heavy hellos

VIII
the body
knees parallel
not knocking
the body
a nude suspension
tied to the nickels tossed on stage.

IX
Divine! Divine!
Dressed to the nines!
Gutter-lovely painting!
Born of the third eye!

X
fly cast
picking through lobster tails
to find the plumpest one.

XI
velvet textured and caked nicotine

> the corner of the bar
> is reserved for the regulars
> is intuitive and growls

XII
the body
thighs: a whirlpool
toes smashed into the foot of heels
the belly, it jumps
cured like split sinew

XIII
and the pole parts the path
to a lily hued pendulum
in motion,
it swings.

cartographer

in an attic
a sour-mashed mappist
making stills
taking note of the winding,
the conviction of points
and the way the land dries up,
a stagnating signal.

lines and divots
cross roads and a loss of space
of highways
and confusion over footing
falling
landing
on the pear in your pocket
a pear sized bruise
you press when you're nervous.

do you see it?
do you see what i'm talking about?
this is where it lives.
this is where it comes from.
do you see it?
do you see what i'm *talking* about?
i made this
from here
and here.
do you see it?
do you see what i'm talking about?
this is the mapping of here and here.

finger-knocking wood
soaked and tepid
into shapes:
archipelago
shapes:
colonial
sodden shapes for intrepids

she sleeps nighttime
dims lamps
sees maps.

three shots gin and a cinnamon stick
sucked and stuck to the roof of the brim

marble mouthed lesions
three beats over the limit
drowned in a brine
aged perimeters
a rumble stomach,
an unmappable mind.

Have you ever seen a girl repaint a map without looking?

dreams are quiet
if you woke to clangor
you would never sleep again
because you cannot map the peal

but the backdrop
it's riddled
a line
a divot
the way you
can dream
people and places
any way you want.

i only liked you
before your papa died
before you
left me
sour,   there's no such thing as lost.
mashed, and mapping.   there's no such thing as loss.

conduit—
can't leave this place until—conduit
a foot or a channel
can
canal
switch the brush to re-paint the ocean.

i've invented oceans.
i've tugged the waves moonless and fed their fish.

can't see strait
a waterway or a way for the water
to lose its space
Babel
reinventing babble
a channel
or a re-re-working of the ocean.

why can't i?
can't i eat the fish from mine—
from my own ocean?

shots to burn through lesions
to burn through skin
mucked up to grime
keeps one lucid
an acute lucidity
a sense of one's own hysteria

three shots gin and a cinnamon stick
sucked and stuck to the roof of the brim

behold
beheld
see india
see books about india, zimbabwe is a country
roads country africa is asia antarctica?
never been.
never seen.
australia never spoke afrikaans
eurasia is australia
is continent is country is
(a pear-size bruise)
goodbye africa
goodbye india
goodbye Olivia
(can't stay awake)
goodbye, daughter went to college in
N – Y – C – N – Y – U – N – E – W
new filament synagogue counties made of cities
made of buildings
and re-buildings of -alities & re-.
i re-ality. i re-build. build i -alities.
i   build.   irelatere—   i   am   maps.

In dreams, you can remember places and people any way you
want. The way your body moved in sync, succinct. You can
remember her oily hair, smell it, feel it through your fingers
and when jilted awake, you can map it. Hysteria is the body
the way you cannot remember it, a refusal to acknowledge
condition and the conditional, the temporary; the body post.

housewife

the skirt only fluffs when you've wrung it through twice.

pour in hot soup to rinse out the wounds
save sap from chopped trees
trees chopped by hands belonging to a man tending fire
while the mother shapes sap into toys for the children.

toys for the children and soup to rinse out wounds,
an infantile comfort.
a comfort which held up
until the children
outgrew the coddle and began chopping wood like their
father.

their father,
a man who walks on all fours,
will shoot a doe from behind
empty its insides
and use its parts for the children.

see, toys made of sap
seldom cross paths with axe-wielding children.

she prepares their meals: a routine,
bows her head on the counter
because she's dizzy
but doesn't miss a beat
when the kettle steams
she thinks
how lovely it would be
to leave
and swim in the ocean all day,

meet a stranger at midnight,
kiss the cleft,
and have him sit funny on a mattress.

like a stranger would at first,
seeing that all new things are funny.
have him lay funny on a mattress
and take love from him.

Is there much else funnier than taking love from a stranger?

a man who proposes marriage in bed is a man who chops
                                                    to build
                                                    to burn
is a man who wraps around the mother like tendrils
but appeals to thorny children
who grow sweet at first
then bitter, uncaring
towards a mother who still kisses scars in company
and squirms at the sight of spoiled meat.

see, the mother (much stranger) cannot crawl
on hands and knees to support the weight of three.

with skirts fluffed and wrung through twice,
lashes fanned and pointing in all the directions she prays to
travel,
to the direction of the ocean,
to the direction of a stranger
who eases towards the surface,
his face speckled with bits
his eyes pleased and pleasing…
a stranger
who eases towards the surface
to lay funny
on a mattress.

Marcella, in wake

from January to March,
the branches hang like rosary
clutched to a covered chest.

at the stop sign,
little peacoats line the sidewalk;
red-tipped, they tremble
huddled and stuck like tinned popcorn.

March through May
the rain beats patterns on the shingles
eyes closed, the visuals:
her mother stirring
pinching dough into clumps
for concrete treats by the fireplace
and her brother,
dressed in cotton,
turning flyers into sailboats
they'll sail nautical
through the puddles after school.

May come June:
she bobs a sodden head to secular gospel
cracks the window
but hesitates to do so
she lays quiet
the kittens panting, wagging their tongues like cubs.

July, August, through Oct—
the walls peel around her
buried in things.

her brother brings necessities:
a carton of milk and cigarettes,
and paints the annual portrait
of Marcella.

she sits curved,
hair hanging down
in fingertwisted ringlets,
nose a corridor to a mouth all fuzz and marble.
hooded lids marked with copper
a rusted homage to their mother.

the children stopped in pairs
paint sweated off from a warm October
their faces painted clown
        painted cat
        painted blue and marbled.

Marcella hung a sign with an arrow
pointed down to a bowl filled with treats
and when morning came,
she pulled back the drape
to find
a single bar untouched.

November, December
the stairs collect dust.

fogged glass reminds her
of her mother's eyes (cast)
nicotine tendrils snaking upward
clouding a face near forgotten.

poor mother,
the way she ate to eat to throw up again.
clots dislodged,
the red pouring forth and coloring the carpet.

and inanimate,
she lay,
in her least favorite dress.

on holidays, Marcella doesn't visit strangers.
her brother rings,
but she doesn't answer,
just works through the cartons
and thinks of her mother.

all bone and tallow,
all chipped and rendered,
and pats the cherry embers
with her least favorite dress.

ARFID
for Patrick Stickles

viciousness in the kitchen!
the television hums
turned up louder
than the grasshopper
outside my window
and I laugh
because my ears are still ringing.

ears abuzz
from standing next to a speaker
ears unplugged
(a masochist? yes.)
and the lead singer,
brother bear,
stretched thin
in sweat-painted pants
screaming:

Patrick Stickles
sick on stage
arms a veined
constellation.
and the fear of food,
the panic!
the heresy!

a knee knobbed
and there are worse adjectives for this:
sinew
stringy
flyblown
on/off the bone.

*

when it's cold
I layer and layer and layer
and still I feel lost
for not even this sea of comfy
can mask the lack of—

I lack shape.
all sticks
and stone soup
in the pit of my belly.

to lift
to drop
to rewind the clock
it's daylight savings time
with no drink to cheers
alone
in a hotel room
with 0
effort
made.

I lack shape,
a pile of mush.
and like dogs,
they dig in,
all paws
with no finesse,
the aroma
streaking chins
vampire red
and they're laughing!
their tongues filmed and flicking!
their green speckled teeth
chaotic in my chest.

If the bulk is animal, I won't.
If the texture is foam, I won't.
If the stem is crunch, I won't.

If the skin is pink,
the smell too green,
                it loses.
the shades cannot enter unless

white rice   cooked
Peter Pan Peanut Butter
Wonder Bread   semolina
white rice cooked
Peter Pan Peanut
Butter
Wonder Bread, semolina
white
rice
cooked
Peter Pan Peanut Butter
Wonder
Bread
semolina
and vegetable broth
prepared so hot
it burns
everything
going
down.

*
little boy of wood
all knots with no splinters
cornered
like a bad boy
like a dunced boy

"I won't, I won't..."

closed off
clammy

"A boy like you ought to grow strong,
ought to force it down, ought to beg for more!"

eyes closed
in slow repetition:
"I won't, I won't..."
mantra
too full from words

vegetable
has too many syllables
and fruit?
all verb and no noun

like:
pear

like:
berry

like:
stalk

the shape of my person
and the logic is flawed
but flaw is my logic

if I look at it
and my stomach flips
if my stomach flips
when I look at it
what will happen

to
it
if
it
enters?
if it
festers?
if it
pushes its way out?

this starvation
is killing me.

*
toss it out
burn the glass
down the sink
it goes
like a wedding ring
silver
diamond
shining
like,
I thought I could love you.
I thought we could come to terms
with this
but your rapid
and your shrinking body
with your brittle
and pale
and silver
it shrieks!
tangled in the teeth
of this illness.